October 3, 2006

Another Year

With sweet lips and tangled tongues, we kissed.
Ah! To reminisce is never to remember.
Feel the glow of an ever burning ember.
The truth was far too hot to hold like this.

Ignoring valid reasons for the valiant escape,
that pain not passion burned the rope free,
and safe inside lies that lust can be,
we waited for Fall to transcend our mistakes.

Now I recline and gaze at the page,
at the words I have written, choices I've made.
Take solace in fact that your debts have been paid.
I move on to the front to face a new age.

Sometime, 2007

The Moon

I sit here staring into space
wondering why I see your face
everywhere I turn
but where am I?
I'm locked inside a morbid maze
of mind and measured better days
just long enough to keep my faith
I recline underneath a velvet sky
Orion plays Cupid tonight,
and I teem with the tide (cont...)

While you were with him,
I was waiting for you
When you lost yourself,
you lost me too
But we're staring at the same moon tonight
and I feel you dreaming of me too
Through the clouds, during these lonely hours,
I miss you... looking at the moon

Ten to, ten after, ten hours, ten days...
ten months, I've been wasting away
waiting for anything to change,
but it can't, and it won't,
so why don't you just leave me alone
It's time
Leave me here to die
Hey, I can see the way
you gaze into my eyes,
and I've never doubted a single word
or a single tear you've cried
But now it's time to say goodbye,
and I hope that you can sympathize
after everything you've put me through
with your selfish alibis

While you were with him,
I was waiting for you
When you lied to me,
you lost me too
But we're staring at the same moon tonight
and I feel you dreaming of me too
Through the clouds, during these lonely hours,
I miss you... looking at the moon

Eucharist

Our Lord Jesus did not say,
"Those who eat of my bread
and who drink of my wine..."

Our Lord Jesus did not say,
"This is like my body,"
or, "This may be my blood."

Our Lord Jesus did not say,
(as His disciples walked away),
"No, that's not what I meant...
They only represent..."

"Do you also want to leave?"
Master, to whom shall we go?
Your Word is eternal life.

July 30, 2008

Life in 100 Words

Life is an arcade. You play games, you get tickets, you cash them in for prizes. There are Praying Games, Service Games, and Suffering Games. You win the most tickets from Suffering Games but no one likes them because they're hard to play and harder to understand. Praying games are the easiest but you have to know what you're doing to win a lot. Service games are easy and you win a bunch of tickets but you have to go out of your way to find them and often you look dumb playing them. Most people stick to bumper cars.

peace

years later, sorry he says
not for her, for the mirror...
what if once it was for her?

long time, no talk, no reason?

once weak knees fallen far to hard to stone floor
hard become hard times
fire become flaming become ashes
quaking ball, rain and no sky,
light above, and stars outside, cried
years and yearns and tries and begs
and hurts and conquers and begs
and dies and rises and dies and begs

all for peace... to offer peace

all for the one day he might meet her maybe
so to say so sorry, so to say not just so many words
so to say not just me, so to say i was i am no more

[aside] two years tried and still i hide

i lied in the grave, died and was saved
i cried i behaved, i loved and i craved
i lost and i caved, i slaved, i bathed,
i raved, i laid and was made to pay the price
almost there... almost there where i can say sincerely
i broke you so i broke myself
i hated you so i hated myself
i lost you so i lost myself
i made you nothing so i made myself nothing

nearly next to nothing i know you don't know

twisted fingertips lips tangled tongue tied crying
run rampant thoughts pictures lies
temptation recreation pool pool table
lists and talks and traps and sins and and and

i knew not... i knew not myself... i knew not no

friend friendly infatuated love loveless love lost
friend love love lost lust death hate hate hate no no no
no no no no no... no

me... it was me

i did it

wow

now i undo it

peace

January 24, 2009

Need Not

We need to need not -
to need nothing but no thing.
Is-ness should be one's business
more than "is this?"
and witness more than
"even if," "unless," or "I wish."

"Can't" can't count
and surely it won't.
Will will will
whether you do or you don't.
You can and you will...
if you will it be so.
Whether she is or is not,
arrives or never shows,
stays or goes,
need not "yes" or "no."
Learn to need not now and know
except by the grace of God you go.

October 17, 2009

On Losing a Child

*And when they saw him they were
astonished; and his mother said to him, "Son, why
have you treated us so? Behold, your father and I
have been looking for you anxiously." And he
said to them, "How is it that you sought me? Did
you not know that I must be in my Father's house?"
(Luke 2: 48-49)*

What sorrow strong you must have met
Whitest Dawn without your son
Fraught with fear in blinding black
Holding hope in child's hand
Fighting fast amidst the throng
Wond'ring what one may have done
T'defend against this darkest day

Where is he?

Carrying on with caravan camels
Playing behind the passing peoples
Flowing on from light to Light
Living just like any other
We were sure he was...
Caught up in the vast commotion
In the din of kin and friends
Lost in life a life is lost
Dare we dream this dream may fade?

Where is He?

Three days long we look and labor
Three days long we pray we fast
Three days long we die and...

Could it be?

Son! We've wept with aching eyes
Too soon lost but now regained!
Why and where and how and... shhh...
Your boy was dead but now he lives
Your son was gone but now he's here
Sweetest Mom, I'm safe and sound
Here at home in Father's house

November 13, 2009

<u>The Trinity in 100 Words</u>

God is that than which nothing greater can be conceived, all-loving and justly deserving of all love. Creation is neither necessary to God's existence, nor eternal, nor capable of infinite love. Only an eternal being capable of infinite love suffices to love God. However, two eternal substances cannot exist separately. Existence alone is eternal; thus, Existence must love Itself selflessly, as one loves another and the latter loves the former. The two Lovers are not love, but begetters of Love, a separate entity consubstantial with the One Substance. Thus, Existence is Lover, Loved, and Love, and the three are one.

March 8, 2011

<u>The Church in 100 Words</u>

As the New Adam slept upon the Cross, his Bride and Mystical Body, the Church, was born from his side, not by water only but by water and blood. At Pentecost, God breathed into her nostrils and she entered into the world, her members baptized into one faith, made one Body by the true food of Christ's flesh, and animated by one Holy Spirit. She is the sacrament of man's inner union with God and the sign and instrument of the Kingdom yet to come. God sends forth from her Christ's mighty scepter until his enemies are made his footstool.

With Morning

The sun comes up in The morning.
sun rises as I do with expectation
for the day we greet With open arms.
above my head, I yawn,
exhaling worries of Yesterday.
doesn't matter anymore
In this new world.
I am free.

Love in Transition [a meditation]

Can we ever be real
I lie here looking on closed eyes two
I kiss lips as soft as any do
You whisper and I listen
You love and I too
We my first my only
In and out twisted up down breathing out in
Skin as supple as any woman's I've ever touched
Hair as conditioned as any I've run fingers through
Voice tinted hint of depth so deep
Resonates in my chest takes away my breath my sleep
Lingering long you fall beautiful upon my pillow-covered arm
Pouch upon my thigh painted nails around my thumb
And I look and caress and think about you and us and me
Why don't I believe
Shadowed eyes covered in dark
Head hung between my legs and yours
Hands behind my head
All eyes looking heavenward
Love outpoured or was it
Love-drunk or was i
Was it for me or for you
For me was it for me or for you
So much effort gone into garnishing that face
Into that smile that walk that embrace
Practiced posture perfect poise
So naturally unnatural
Who's to say you're not what you are
Or that you are what you're not
No one
Even you

What to say when you say you're as much a woman as they
So what you have this or that
You run with the ball go to bat with the best
Though you pound that proudly pillowed chest
It will give suck but never nourish
And what of I
I who thirsted so I drank you in
I who wanted this not that
I who said I can love whom I want
But am not free not to want
Can it be said I love her for her
Or him for him
If the choice is made before I begin
She's perfect because she's the type to which I can't say no
Now I pour out my pants and hold on tight to the one who slides
A little closer a little further every moment
Whom I'm into and can't get out of
Do I love you or do I love the chains that won't break
That bind me behind and before and about the waist
Can I kiss these lips and really say I love you
Or do I love me

February 22, 2015

Maranatha! Lord, come and be with me
because I can't see much farther
than this lamp upon my feet—
just enough light to take another step
just enough life to take another breath
I'm so tired of having to choose
of fighting the flesh and wanting to lose
I come outside and yell at the sky
as if this feeling is your fault not mine

April 16, 2015

Lord, no one ever told me
that growing old would be this hard
Granted, I'm only 28,
but things haven't gone so well thus far
Every dream I've ever had
has stayed stuck within my head
And every talent that you gave
is buried behind my bed somewhere
Jesus, just this once,
let me open my mouth and sing
Maybe just one person will hear this song
and in that moment decide to live, decide to live

Lord, I'd be a liar if I said I'm proud of me
I don't want to leave this life
with hands as soft and empty as these
By your grace and with your help
I'll do what we can't do by ourselves
All is well and all will end well
Come what may, I won't be afraid, I won't be afraid

God, I'm not so good at this game
but I won't quit, so I play
that maybe this music
will bring a smile to your face
Lord, you are the narrow rocky way
that I love, so I pray
that everyone will come
and make this journey
what it's meant to be, what it's meant to be

October 24, 2015

The Good Shepherd

[I] live in fear of stifling what's beautiful in you
Cowering before the question, my heart aches
Should I sit you in rows, press you to speak only when spoken to
or preserve what is yet childlike in you
Should I allow your obedient mischief because it will nowhere else
be tolerated
be a bit too slack because everywhere else the world will be taught
with all those maxims that make a man into a machine
which make a free spirit a cynic
which make an innocent heart jaded
which make a kid an adult
Sure, I can fit you into rows like eggs
so you can sit and hear everything I say
and copy it down word for word like some surrogate Gospel
or I can grasp a bit more loosely
so that when I say something worth saying
you will not only hear but understand
and you will want to understand
because your heart is in my hand
Somewhere ages and ages hence
when we happen upon each other in the marketplace
you with your own kids in tow
I hope to see that glint of mischief in your eye
unextinguished

Valentine

Valentine
O shining starlet!
I can see you in the night sky,
but you don't know I'm here.
That's okay;
I'll sing so maybe you can hear what you can't see.
See,
and raise a toast to what might be.
Will you be my Valentine this year?
Will you be my Valentine this year?
The New York snow is a little too cold to bear alone
(for me).
We can dream can't we?
Just last week, I was singing a song in my car.
I went to give you a call…
(sigh)
Have you ever missed someone you've never met before?
I think I do.
I think it's you…
When my heart sings,
I just let it do its thing.
I can't help that you're my muse;
these are not the type of things we choose.
[The song I was singing in my car:]
By the by, girl, will you be my Valentine?
Will you let me call you mine,
even if only this one time?
I know with that smile
you must be in high demand.
I won't pretend that I don't know that,
but you're worth the one-in-a-million chance.
Oh yeah.

[part of an impromptu haiku battle]

Aidan ***
thinks he can out-haiku me.
Where are my green slips?

April 17, 2016

<u>Happy Birthday</u> [a song]

Maybe we'll go to California—
impromptu road trip
We can drive all night—
a few friends and you and I—
in my Chevy with you riding shotgun
singing to a playlist of our songs
On the highway, we'll race the sunrise
Summer break will never end…
Happy birthday, girl!
Life's a little bit different than last year, I know…
but I hope you never grow up
and that smile never fades
from your face
Let's be kids for just another few decades, please
We were in such a rush to grow up
Now, we have the car keys
We can drive all night—
or stop to watch the stars go by
The rules are ours to make
Opportunities are ours to take
We are young…
we are heroes…
and summer break will never end (cont…)

There's no time to waste
We've finally found the place
Where time flew
from all those better days
Let's go make it home
and play there all day long
with the ones we love
and take our time before it's gone…

May 8, 2016

Songs from Ocean Parkway - Track 1 [a song]

Whatcha thinkin, lady,
as you look into the blue?
Will you tell me secrets?
Are you peeking at me
from inside your hoodie?
Maybe this is just a game…just a dream…
Catching the sun between our fingers,
feet resting on the horizon at Long Beach,
from our bench-seats upon the boardwalk—
there's still something too far to reach
In your glasses, I see the ocean
Through them, I see open wide a way to know you
as deep as the backlit sky
Catching the moon between our fingers,
feet resting on the cool starlight of Long Beach,
from our theater seats upon my car hood—
there's still one heart too far to reach
There's an ocean between your world and mine—
an abyss we can abridge in time… time…
When the twain shall meet,
we'll build a lighthouse there,
and we'll never be lost again

See the sunrise in the east? It is so beautiful,
and I confess that I can hardly contain myself at all
I feel like I'm going to fly away
Would you come with me?
In this moment worth a movie,
I think we ought to celebrate
And if I sound too over-elated,
it's understated compared to how I feel
I would tell tell the world that you and I are free
I pinch myself to see if the reverie is real for me…
I wish you were here

Holy Thursday, 2017

Self-knowledge

Thus I begin another notebook
wondering if this time
I will finish

Beauty

God, I met a girl
outwardly adorned with
earrings and chin clefts
and glasses and round lips–
an introvert who caught me looking and liked it
I don't question whether she'd go out tonight
but rather how she'd look from inside

Haiku 2

God, how things have changed
Clouds used to bring us to you
iClouds, not so much

Easter Wednesday, 2017

A Story Not Yet True

Son, why are you in a sleeping bag
in a Jeep in a Walmart parking lot?
The man was threatening my life, sir,
so I came here to save myself.

Epiphany

Never once
though a million times I'd seen
had I ever seen
the elevated train in the sunset
of the McDonald's parking lot

I see a tree,
but you would see
the inadequacy of my words

Easter Thursday, 2017

Some say that,
when at a loss for time
one
has to
make it
Since that is impossible, .
I recommend
we
take it

Ashen cares washed away—
a cloud kissed my neck
on the porch.

I had given up on resolutions
but today
This will be a ten-minute shower
so I can have a five-minute cup of coffee
before getting to work five minutes early, and then…

Twenty-minute shower
I give up on resolutions

I had given up on resolutions
but today
I'm going to make my bed
because when I make my bed
I feel in control of life,
whereas when I don't,
I feel as if my life is in disarray, and…

I'm late for work
I give up on resolutions

Divine Mercy Sunday, 2017

Olivia Munn

Sometime, [I] will see
a bulb waiting to blossom
alone in a library
Pray that I welcome you
into A world without.
ulterior motives

April 24, 2017

Buried Treasure

To which banker should I go?
None has earned my interest.

Amy Schumer

If I had let me love you,
we wouldn't be so lost.
My broken heart won't work,
and yours won't hold my love.

April 25, 2017

I let the rain ruin my hair,
and a tree appeared in full flower.

Haiku 3

I'm thirty years old.
I hope I'll know what to do.
At this point, she will.

In a parallel universe,
I wouldn't be I.

Perception

What a strange and disgusting fruit.
Oh, it's an ice-filled glass viewed from above.

                    May 3, 2017

This time

Today
I can say with certitude
that I've never known much of anything
but I believe like a stubborn child
that everything is going to be alright
this time

Psalm 88

Thy Known and
as truck meter
mend us blows
endtimes tilled
rye into un-durst and
y.

May 14, 2017
Mother's Day

The Chaminade Man
does not write
a poem entitled "Aunt Jemima"—
although now would be the right time
(with so few of us watching)

From Now On

[i] saw a unique tree
in front of some house on Broadway
becoming so beautiful.
It did what it could,
and did it well.
Many sparrows chose to live in its leaves.
It gave shade, gave example,
and mattered.

Sunday, May 21, 2017

Moving Out

Living in my parents' house
was ne'er an issue until now
I lost my job and realized
my issues became theirs somehow

Haiku 4

Is this poetry?
It's not about anything—
but I'm living it.

Brandon Boyd

Alliterated name
fame by happenstance
hair, smile, glance
tattoos that tell stories
songs that sing
voice in free verse
He paints with words
surfs the world on watercolors
but his heart is in the stars
Take a picture
Be grateful

May 24, 2017
Solemnity of Our Lady Help of Christians (Australia)

Fifty years hence,
no one will remember
whether I bent to the windswept whims of my parents
pandering for approval written in sand
Perhaps no one will think well of me
even if I did things never done before
I'm not saying that I am dust
so I might as well be dirty
I am saying that
You are water and rock, so
We might as well build something beautiful

Haiku 5

Rain! Lord, make it rain.
Let me know things wash away.
Make me remember.

Haiku 6

The sun peaks through clouds
Suddenly all is beauty
Stop lying to me

Haiku 7

For what do I long?
If home is where the heart is,
no wonder I'm lost.

Driving through the fog
on Ocean Parkway
headed east toward Captree,
I wonder if the view
is more beautiful than it's ever been
Perhaps if I could see farther ahead,
I would call it a metaphor

May 28, 2017

Why guard my backpack as it sits on the boardwalk beside me?
Why so quick to snap a pic of the blue fish slowly dying?
Why do I look so long at the girl whose face I cannot see?

…all for the same reason maybe

Haiku 8

His car's bass thunders
such that one can hardly think.
Scratch that—I meant two.

Sitting in my car at Captree
with windows somewhat open
I feel a Pentecost coming
Oh, whisper after the storm, after the fire,
call me ignorant
call me foolish
call me what you will as I wait for you
        but
        call me

                    May 31, 2017

Chaminade was not a job from which I was fired
It was not a family from which I was ostracized
She was a woman to whom I made love—
to whom I gave everything—
and she rejected me

June 10, 2017

Sometimes,
I feel like an unborn child
and the womb is not mine
Voices say "Welcome home"
but I'm all alone
and I know nothing nor anyone
Where do I belong
If not here?
I fear there's nowhere I belong
or
that I belong
nowhere

June 16, 2017

Haiku 9

I can write haiku
without even trying to.
Heck! Here's one right now.

One Way or the Other

Bullet shell of a being,
fast and empty in your dealing,
who pierce and proclaim healing,
fire-and-brimstone while you can.

From where does the fruit fly descend,
and how does it know the scent,
that when something sweet is left,
it comes to devour it?

Vulture, fallen angel,
who consume the innocent,
I hope your hunger devours itself,
and when it's done

there's nothing left.

June 20, 2017

Don't let dreams   pass you by
She caught my eye—
blonde with a bulldog nose ring
tattoo on her arm
tan Wrangler driving
down Nassau Blvd.
Don't look in the rearview closely
Yet here am I

Life

They hurried away
huddled with hoods up
as I walked toward the boardwalk
One can enjoy the rain
only if she is prepared to get wet
Then, it can be beautiful

In Thought

I walked out of the house
with a smile on my face
and said to unknowing parents,
"See you later"
I was wearing shorts I consider pajamas
I was procrastinating with loads of schoolwork
I was going to my secret spot on the beach

I'm glad that, in the midst of a world
that seeks to rob us of solitude,
there is still one place
where a man can be alone

  know that someth ng s m ss ng,
but can't qu te f gure out what t s...

June 21, 2017

Haiku 10

Lonely as I am,
I really need a restroom—
funny how that works.

Haiku 11

I see you alone
and hesitate to intrude.
Would you want me to?

Haiku 12

Do I fear the one,
or just every not-the-one?
It's so hard to tell.

Who made the diva,
and why do we need her—
the pretentious, whining woman
who thinks the world is her theater?

Unku 1

Now I know
why people pay
to feel less alone

June 22, 2017

The Battle for Long Beach [a meditation]

Clouds accumulate
like battleships in blockade—
a siege laid by heaven
on the world we've made
The sky doesn't want
shops and high-rises
brightly-lit bars and advertisements

And every so often it reminds us

Would that we could yearly rebuild the ties that bind us
and surrender to heaven before it finds us

Unku 2

Stand right there
Forget your hair
Just enjoy the rain

June 24, 2017
St. John the Baptist

Yes, it's majestic,
but not tonight…
Tonight, the sky is the vast empty,
and I'm alone
in the beautiful nothing

The half moon waits
to be made whole
The world will move
to make it so

June 25, 2017

Lorde

I've known you for a minute and a half
It was a great song
Let's just leave it at that

I've known you for a minute and a half
Now, I long to be that friend
to whom you show unfinished tracks

whom you text when lights go black
who hides when he looks at your hair
Let's just leave it at that

I've known you for a minute and a half
but if I knew you at all
would your voice still call me back?

Perhaps my dream would collapse…
and I've been hurt too many times
Let's just leave it at that

Or worse…you're perfect for me—
and then what…we'll never meet?
I've known you for a minute and a half
Let's just leave it at that

July 2, 2017

Colored Boy in a Rough Neighborhood

An 18-year-old prep school boy
was walking through the hall—
articulate, responsible,
respected well by all.
"All Ivy Leagues have chosen him,"
read Newsday's exposé.
Accepting cheers with eloquence,
"I'm humbled," he would say…

An 18-year-old Freeport boy
I hadn't seen in years
was walking with two friends of his.
Their words were quite unclear.
A gang had chosen him,
and it's tattoos were on his neck—
the type that earn a bullied boy
an ounce of false respect.

One rose above the boundaries
that people make of skin,
and one became the colored boy
in order to fit in.

July 8, 2017

Tonight

I need

to hear

your heart

July 9, 2017

Unku 3

Loneliness
is so silent...
I need your music

July 12, 2017

<u>Tal</u>

, This is the most satisfied I've ever been with myself
but when work ends I remember

I need someone else

Music and poetry have always gone together
and fame has always been the luck of the draw
I guess what I'm trying to say is
you and I might not be far apart after all
I mean…
I mean…

I wish you were here

But come quick if you come at all
Already I can feel me forcing myself not to dream
You are a jazz club in the city
and as with so many I've seen
I may visit once and give up
refusing to believe that I'm enough—
just romantic and foolish
trusting but broken
beautiful and better off   alone

What is it I'm searching for in you?
What is it I hope you have?
I want…
I want…

love

, James

Haiku 13

I need to know you—
if only so we can say,
"This could never be"

The clock like a mourner
with hands on its face
keeps ticking and turning,
the earth keeping pace.

And likewise my heart
keeps beat with bad timing.
I'd stop me from falling
while you're still crying.

But I'm like your tears
in more ways than this—
I'm warm and transparent,
a salve for the lips.

Like salt in a wound
healing and burning.
Maybe it's best
that the world won't stop turning.

Haiku 14

It's been fifteen years
I hope you don't want me yet
I'm still not ready

Unku 4

I could cry
I should be better
And I would with you

Haiku 15

I fell in the dark
I had been looking for you
But you weren't there

Haiku 16

Someone tell Basho
these are about nature too—
but that of humans

July 23, 2017

Unku 5

No high heels
No more makeup
Just jeans and t-shirts

July 24, 2017
St. Charbel

Haiku 17

Mondays after school
Volleyball at Cedar Beach
Summer comes early

Haiku 18

With her in the dark
I will always remember
how lonely I was

July 26, 2017

Sunrise at Montauk

Mother Earth gives birth to the sun
Water breaks on the shore of the ocean
I want to be there with you
as the red sky burns into blue

July 28, 2017

Haiku 19

Clouds from a tea cup–
the world was moving quickly,
but now it stands still.

July 29, 2017
St. Martha

mile
own lean s
isn't say she a bull
eye
can't duet bye
mice hell
Floored

August 1, 2017

Sometimes I drive down Marlboro
to consult the ghost of Ed Burns—
to ask how he plans
to pitch that flick to Robert Redford.
I say, "Wow, bro, you're wild.
No one gets famous that way."
He says, "No, no one yet,
but who are you to take my chances?"
I grin, "Hey, how does this sound—
me building a life out of guitars?"
He says, "It sounds like rock n' roll, man,
and you're among the stars."

August 2, 2017

Haiku 20

Do what you love. Die.
Or do what you hate…Still die.
Why do we conform?

August 3, 2017

Haiku 21

I'm giving up now;
it was a stupid idea.
She'll be better off?

Haiku 22

Tell me I must wait…
Tell me seven thousand years…
I would wait for her.

Unku 6

No poems…
Too dark tonight…
Don't poison the page

Haiku 23

Few things sadden me
like a beautiful woman
as she passes by

Unku 7

Hope, perhaps
should take more space
than my despair does

Unku 8

Read me red
Between my lines
I'm an open wound

August 10, 2017

Unku 9

vanity:
vapid beauty
ugly irony

August 11, 2017

Haiku 24

If you would have me
let's make music together
(a world for our love)

Haiku 25

I don't understand.
I'm supposed to be sorry,
but did I do wrong?

August 12, 2017

I fear straight people
who say I'm a homophobe
for being Catholic

Unku 10

So, old friend,
you haven't left—
inadequacy

Haiku 26

A late august day
Driving into the sunset
A new apartment

Haiku 27

O cruel Twilight
why consume the lonely heart
with raging beauty

Haiku 28

Selling shirts for cash
Bootstrapping in a basement
Hats off for freedom

Haiku 29

They're not so pretty
They could be better arranged
But they are my own

Sometime, 2017

Laura Mvula—
that's how you say it, right?
You're a big star, I hear...
but not here.
In this space
U and I
are the same size
And as characters in a bigger picture
aren't we all

small

Yet your music affects mine
and ours others
in a way that transcends
time
and leaves space   behind
So that we sing together
with ones we've never met
and our chorus resounds
after the universe

goes quiet...

September 7, 2017

I've been a bad boy...
stockings around my neck
lump of coal in my throat
I'm stuck in your fishnets
with all the others in this boat
I'm peering through the screen
suffocating in my need
There are other fish in here
but you're the one I want to feed
tonight

You've been a bad girl…
face framed like a picture—
a painted image on a desk
I know it isn't really you
but I admire like the rest
We mouth empty words
stare with unblinking eye
You came online to draw us in
but we all came to die
hooked

September 15, 2017

Creativity
takes so many letters
from "patient" and "lucky"

September 30, 2017

Welcome to the West End—
a beautiful face
where everyone knows
your first name

October 3, 2017

Haiku 30

The power of thought—
I'll pretend I don't want you
Soon it will be true

October 11, 2017

Haiku 31

Everyone matters
A homeless street performer
made me feel again

Haiku 32

Remember, children,
it's not about the money
It's about beauty

October 12, 2017

Haiku 33

Yay surrogacy
This isn't what he ordered
He wants two, not three

October 15, 2017

Haiku 34

It's too soon she said
I wish he would respect that—
he and every man

Haiku 35

If girls only knew
how deeply lonely I am
I'd have many friends

Haiku 36

He says certainly,
"She's the best I've ever had,"
who waits for his wife

November 17, 2017

Last week, I cried about my ex-fiancée
But it's been three years since the day
I don't know if that's touching or strange or what
I didn't cry when we broke up
Not for her sake anyway
It's weird how things work out that way

There was a party
I wonder if I was missed
If I was looked for

When one is lonely
Everyone is beautiful
Every one but me

Billy Joel

One with music in his heart must sing.
It is a sacred task—
not for fame,
not for money,
but for the heart that hears.
Because every song
has a lover to whom it whispers—
a soul that it knows
more deeply than any friend.
And the writer is a priest
who brings messages from the nothing
to those that need them.

Unku 11

Memento
All people die
Not all will have lived

December 10, 2017

Unku 12

Fatalists—
born of failure
to take what we want

December 12, 2017

I want to lie with you in truth
I want you to find my scars
We will bear our nakedness
We will bear all things

December 14, 2017

Haiku 37

Transgenderism—
A circular argument
We used to know that

December 17, 2017

Unku 13

IVF
We love our kid
And killed the others

December 19, 2017

Haiku 38

Her clothes are so hot
Nakedness could not compare
What a travesty

December 26, 2017

Dancer
so visceral
my reaction to your art
years ago
to this day
I haven't had the heart
even to seek your name
Yes, I had seen dance
but once
I felt it

January 13, 2018

Between "I don't deserve this"
and "She doesn't deserve that"
is a safe place
not big enough for two

Haiku 39

Her eyes are half closed,
and her legs are half open—
a poor way to search

February 17, 2018

Unku 14

Of ourselves
We know little
Others must teach us

Haiku 40

Grace not energy
Gratitude not contentment
Mercy not karma

February 18, 2018

Unku 15

Sad but true
To be human
Is to make mistakes

Unku 16

She's so odd
That's what I like
What I should resist

February 20, 2018

Unku 17

When you pass
I close my eyes
I'm a non-starter

March 30, 2018

Unku 18

I'm so sad
So don't ask me
I won't let you in

May 3, 2018

Unku 19

Gemini,
Stars don't move you
Just ask the magi

May 20, 2018

Haiku 41

I wish you were here,
my love, whoever you are.
Have I met you yet?

May 28, 2018

The romance of the Eucharist
Is so beautiful
That even those who don't believe
Would wish it were true
If they merely knew

Haiku 42

Beautiful places
Overrun by the richest
While the poor still dream

Unku 20

Dear Dana
It hurt to leave
I hope you know that

July 3, 2018

Haiku 43

Child-like purity:
a valueless novelty
Hanging on a cross

July 4, 2018

I am where ulterior motives go to die

August 22, 2018

Unku 21

Cyanide
Sayonara
Why even bother

August 12, 2018

Perfect love casts out all fear
That makes sense
Because I'm so afraid
That I can't love

August 14, 2018

When I get into bed
I'm the loneliest man I've ever met

August 29, 2018

If I wasn't Christian
I'd be gone
If I wasn't holy
There would be a hole in me

November 1, 2018

I don't think anyone will love me
And why should she
If I'm not who I should be?

December 26, 2018

It's the age of the pro-choice vegan
I wish you were all just cannibals
So I could know what you stand for

January 1, 2019

Feel free
To underestimate me
I will prove you wrong

March 23, 2019

Haiku 44

In the living room
A dead man watches tv
I never knew him

May 30, 2019

Am I a creep
Or just desperately alone
Or both
Who knows

June 2, 2019

Between letting go
I can never find the line
And not caring at all

July something

What's the point of catharsis
when you have no one to share the art with?

My fantasies used to be outrageous stuff.
Nowadays, a hug is enough.
Man, that's depressing, huh?
G*d, I just want to be loved.

It's been five years this month
that I proposed to the girl I loved.
Should I burn this box of stuff,
or spend this life beating myself up?

I'm lonely and tired and getting old.
I don't know if I want love anymore.
I mean, of course I do, sure,
but I've lost it too many times before.

Unku 22

Wash; brush; shave;
stretch; eat; smile; breathe...
Why? There's no one here.

Every picture is of her shell.
Is there anyone in there?

August 2, 2019

Haiku 45

Even dead bees sting
Think about your legacy
Don't let it be sin

August 11, 2019

Thankfully the plaster
was the same color as the wall
But maybe I shouldn't
have punched it at all

August 14, 2019

"We begin tonight's episode
with a murder-suicide in Bed-Stuy."
Wow, do you see the reporter's shirt?
It doesn't even match his tie!
Yes, honey, he clearly should've worn blue.
What is the world coming to?

August 24, 2019

Life is a constant struggle
Not to hate God
For the work of the devil

August 25, 2019

It's none of my business
Until you're closing my cake shop

August 28, 2019

Haiku 46

Pangs of loneliness—
Better than being in love
And watching it break

August 30, 2019

Haiku 47

I'm a Catholic
You don't realize what I said
If you didn't gasp

September 18, 2019

Unku 23

In my eyes
You see despair
But judge it malice

September 19, 2019

Unku 24

How much proof?
A bleeding host?
The sun crashing down?

Unku 25

Foolish heart
Open your doors
Let in love again

<u>M.T.</u>

Wow, that girl with no hair or eyebrows is beautiful.
Yes, we are aren't we?
Yes, you are.
Aren't we beautiful, girls, just the way we are?!
[confused]
We are so beautiful, and no one can tell us we're not!
…
Let's get half-naked and pose to prove it.
Why?
And these are our new wigs!
But…
And LGBT!
Huh??
Aren't we beautiful?! Call me They!
No.
Call me They, dammit!
…You're a freak.

September 20, 2019

<u>Haiku 48</u>

Beyond my borders
There is a type of person
Who can unlock me

September 22, 2019

<u>Haiku 49</u>

By today's standards
Christ was not very Christ-like
So Christians should bow.

September 24, 2019

Sasha Luss

When I'm not snorting images like coke
The screen is a mirror and my eye is sound
There's nothing I wanted less
than to see your chest tonight
Because you're my sister
and I love you.

September 26, 2019

I'm awake now
It's a metaphor
I'm not sure what for

September 27, 2019

Haiku 50

Talented people—
Why do they get paid the most
For their unearned gifts

September 28, 2019

I childproofed my phone
Because I'm a man

September 30, 2019

I always fart when I'm the most sad
Thanks, God
I thought we were having a moment

Always telling half-truths
Go find an FTM who grew a set
or who walked a mile and then turned back

Heresy, sweet heresy
I told myself I wouldn't write this song
but what's done is done
A box of memories is full
and five years later I can't burn it yet
I was on my knees when I found you
I was praying when I put my arms around you
Heresy, sweet heresy…
Do whatever your heart tells you
Follow what you feel
No one said it wasn't real
That God wasn't in my gut
So we fell deeper and deeper
Crazy and crazier in love
And I with the hand of God above
put the ring upon your finger
Because I felt so led
Because it's what the Spirit said…
Heresy, sweet heresy
And because I thought I had no choice
but to listen to that evil voice
confused though I was
I ran into what I wasn't ready for
What a hard lesson to learn– (cont…)

that sometimes God speaks
but mostly just wants us to choose
Heresy, sweet heresy
that destroyed us
but let me love you

I have odd songs in my heart
Songs that no one understands
But when I sing them you will

2200 corpses in a basement
The nightly news is silent
But a mother weeps in her car
Knowing her baby was in a jar

Sometimes the shortest path
To where you want to be
Is starting over
So let's do that...you and me.

Unku 26

I'm trapped here
Trusting in you
Do not forsake me

October 26, 2019

Be wholly like him
Exitus et reditus
Be holy like him

October 28, 2019

That pedestal is like a ledge

October 29, 2019

I imagine heaven
as a state of being
where everyone gets
the apology they used to need
and gives the forgiveness
they used to hoard
where everyone knows
Mr. Rogers is a saint
and also decides
to live like he did
where people come
to hear my heart
because they know
it's beautiful like theirs
and people can cry all day
because of how happy they are
but they forget to
because they're so happy

November 15, 2019

Haiku 51

Girls wear half clothing
But they don't know it's missing
So they won't find it

January 3, 2020

Grecian Skies
I'll never be enough for you
And I know that
But I'm nice to have around
I searched for you in San Jose
In LA
You weren't in Long Beach or Lake Grove
Grecian skies
You rebuilt me
Now I'm mighty Atlas on bended knee
Who under   stands
I save who saved me
And I'll hold you up until I collapse
Although you'll never hold me back

February 24, 2020

He hands her the remote
As if to ask
Was it as good for you as it was for me
And she smiles in return
Because after decades
She's learned to fake it

March 2, 2020

She can have anyone she wants
Except me

March 14, 2020

Haiku 52

Even after years
There is no way I could learn
My palms' rivulets

March 19, 2020

Haiku 53

In order to feel
Girls who don't believe in love
Turn to violence

March 24, 2020

Haiku 54

I live in a world
of unattractive beauty—
of grandeur abused

March 31, 2020

If a prophet told me
We'd meet when we were ninety
And we'd be together for one day
I'd wait anyway

Years in advance
You planned a romantic vacation
For your one-and-only
Saving every penny you could
To lavish your love on her
But the week before
She planned an orgy
And you weren't invited
You were both going to be
the best you've ever had
But now you will always be
Just one among many
the mediocre and boring
The one with the learning curve
The I've-had-better
The it's-all-the-same-to-me
The you'll-never-satisfy-me
    And that's what it feels like
    To be a virgin at thirty-three

I miss you like a lover
and that's why I won't write
Because you don't deserve that
But that's just how I feel tonight
Maybe in the morning
I'll see things in a different light
And you and I will be compatible
But that's just how I feel tonight

Everyone's so touch and go
These days
How about we touch and stay
And touch

April 13, 2020

Garabandal
When sins are revealed—
When consciences are laid bare—
Will people repent
Or call God a tyrant

April 18, 2020

I'm publishing my heart in a book.
Wow, I'd love to read it when it's done.
Actually it is done. Here it is!
Oh cool... I'll look at it eventually,
but here's a beautiful picture of me for you!
Oh wow, just for me?!
I mean I put it on Facebook first...
Oh... thanks.

April 20, 2020

I'm good for saying nice things
And the wrong thing
Successively
You can count on me

May 6, 2020

Haiku 55

Turn off the TV
Maybe you'll hear me screaming
Or maybe you won't

Content creator
You're a porno playing piano
As if you weren't good enough

Haiku 56

Sit on sofa thrones
Judge television pictures
Damn hypocrisy

Haiku 57

I am her best friend
But she's just an acquaintance
Who has no idea

Unku 27

I cage it
Then it escapes
A hole in the wall

June 24, 2020

I wish someone could convince me
Not to be Christian
But then I'd wish
Those who indoctrinated me
Would burn in hell

July 2, 2020

I could've loved you forever
Or whatever

July 27, 2020

Haiku 58

Love is a hammer—
An attack on weakened knees
That induces kicks

July 31, 2020

Yvette

This is such a strange conversation
I was trying to thank you
For the good you've done me
But you looked right through
At someone else
And no matter what I would've said
You'd have thought I was he
And you weren't entirely wrong
Because once I was

August 8, 2020

Haiku 59

They open their mouths
I hear Darth Vader speaking
"This is CNN"

October 30, 2020

Haiku 60

Yes, we're together
A perfect pair of scissors
And two halves make holes

November 24, 2020

Unku 28

"But I can't"
True, if you won't
If not now, then when

January 6, 2021

I will never be inside you
Or you inside me
So why try
Yet
New life
Can come forth
From the mere attempt

Unku 29

Sticks and stones
Will build my walls
Guarded and alone

Haiku 61

Hanging in twilight
Around the tabernacle
Dust like galaxies

Unku 30

What is fame?
A cruel hoax
The forging of gods

Teenagers at Captree

The condensation
is gone from their windows—
drops as of sweat
raining like manna
running like fugitives
vanishing into air
hiding mistakes
made like love
in a car that can't drive far enough
The calm after the storm
settles upon hearts in wonder
that wonder

February 13, 2021

Haiku 62

We create people
And make them suffer on screens
For our enjoyment

February 14, 2021

Unku 31

Brevity—
God speaks one Word,
and so two should we

February 17, 2021

I travel back in time
With gift to atone
He stares at me
And I at him
Forgetting what's real
Forgetting the present

February 18, 2021

Everything is self-evident
To one who knows everything

February 21, 2021

Haiku 63

All of a sudden
I saw how many I'd lost
Because I got mad

March 2, 2021

Saints Jerome and Augustine, help me
I received the chastity I prayed for
And it's ugly as sin

To me, love was never a game
Perhaps that's why it was never fun

March 3, 2021

we have chosen you as Vice President
[in order to elevate black women
above
dehumanization and objectification]
not primarily because of your qualifications
but because a white male needed
someone female and black to serve
under
him.

Haiku 64

How are these my hands?
I would not have chosen these
Yet still they are mine

God of rings
God of power
I've been thinking
of two towers
My eye
has raised each to heaven
But I can't build either at this hour

March 5, 2021

Haiku 65

I am a Christian
Great is my desolation
Greater is my hope

March 7, 2021

I keep reaching for the box cutter
Because it was the safety knife that cut me
It was the safety knife that cut me

Haiku 66

I pray this for you
May you be so ignorant
As to escape fire

Lord, open my heart to them
Rip open the cage that imprisons it
Pierce it
Let it bleed for them
Amen.

March 24, 2021

<u>Unku 32</u>

More than sex
I want someone
Who understands me

Faintly from across the chasm
I heard porn stars crying
Prisoner, save yourself
From the trap we set

March 28, 2021

<u>Unku 33</u>

Palm Sunday
You can rejoice
Despite the future

The more I hear about fame
The more I know its peril
But I can't remember for long enough
Not to want it

April 3, 2021

There isn't a single girl
Who won't get old
If she lives long enough

April 4, 2021

I haven't worked all week
But I won't ruin Sunday too
Suffer through the comfort
Work tomorrow

April 5, 2021

The smaller a family becomes
The weirder it gets

April 9, 2021

Some messengers
Make Christ all things to all people
But the Christs they make can't save

April 10, 2021

I have a t-shirt
I wear it to show off my arms
It's getting old now

April 11, 2021

Things are only dead so long
Then they are dust
And find their way back to life
In another form

April 21, 2021

Females once were
Everything they try to be
But now I'm quite desensitized
By their practiced perfection
So if they want to screw someone
They can screw themselves
For ruining something
So special

April 27, 2021

Why is there so much suffering and death in the living room?
It may as well be the dining room with how you devour it
Perhaps that excrement belongs in the bathroom
Or the fiery darkness of the ancient basement
But you store it with relish in the attic of your minds
And who knows where or when it will be unboxed
I wish you were outside

May 9, 2021

Strangers in fiction
That you care about
No-ones doing nothing
In a plastic box
As your children watch

May 10, 2021

No one I've truly trusted and respected
Has ever had to tell me to smile more
Or loosen up

The blood of Januarius
Half liquified in his presence
It's the half that didn't which worries me

May 24, 2021

Whatever it was
That I didn't write down
Would've helped many

May 29, 2021

God remembers
The childhood of earth
How things used to be
Very good
For He so loves the world

May 30, 2021

My comforter
Has been a good friend

Unku 34

Paralyzed
By fear of death
He died ev'ry day

June 9, 2021

We all said, What a jerk
When my co-worker walked out
A good man
My boss asked him, Why

July 9, 2021

Haiku 67

Among many lies
Are some who embrace you back
And drag a soul down

July 20, 2021

Women used to be special
But didn't notice
So they made themselves more special
Adding dyes and powders
Gestures and glances
Perfume and adornments
Pills and IUDs
Until anyone could be as special they are
Even men

On August 31st
I missed the 7pm ferry to Fire Island
and thought the summer was over

Little did I know

that I would eat at Nicky's for the first time
and take the 8:30 under warm starlight

Three years ago
I thought I'd never see another year…

as good as this one

September 2, 2021

Haiku 68

Thanks, Christian neighbor
For running away from me
Rather than say hi

September 22, 2021

Empty
Shells amid the waves
Sifted upon the strand
Not so much dead as abandoned
Twisted and hollow
Or hard and broken
Aimlessly stabbing at soles
Longing to be touched
And worn and thrown away
Impossible to repair
But listen to them whisper
Begging for rebirth

September 28, 2021

I would've worked diligently
To earn that body
But you gave it to me free of charge
And robbed it of its worth

October 5, 2021

I want to give my lips
To someone who doesn't deserve me

October...18, 2021

My world is full of feelings that I don't understand
I don't even know what day it is
Although I've been trying to keep track
If you told me to map out the freckles on my arm
I couldn't, although I've seen them every day for years
That's why I am surprised sometimes
When I look in the mirror
Because we never know what we will see
I've wanted to know you so badly
It occasionally drives me to tears
And yet I'd rather know you in another world
Where pieces become whole
Where I can't mess it up
Here, I'd rather be alone
All I know about you are the expressions of your face
Your fidelity to your friends
The songs you listen to when you're sad
I don't know you
Or me

October 22, 2021

I am not worthy to serve
But
Am I so unworthy
As to be exempt?

October 25, 2021

It's a sickness
That when others tell us we're beautiful
It's not enough
Because we don't believe it

November 3, 2021

Television is his whole life
But if you ask him what he's watching
He would say I don't know

Oftentimes I'd like to stop life
And admire a tree to my heart's content
As when I was a child
I'd sit in the shower
Reading the mystical ingredients on the shampoo bottle
Until someone remembered the water was running

Let's not make this
Harder than we have to
It's only been five minutes
But I think we're done here

The pain
That we can have sex
But I'll never be inside you

November 5, 2021

My heart is a liberal
Walking a beat to the left
But my brain is always right
Right

I hope I'm suffering for you
And not merely because of you

Unku 35

Please, lovely
Don't dare touch me
I'm not worth your time

November 9, 2021

Tell me everything about you
But start with the worst things
Make me want to leave

November 13, 2021

The world is a phase

November 16, 2021

[a meditation]
I went ahead
And found a gun
I blew away
Into wind
Like a favor
Like an old friend
Like the undead
I returned
To end you

November 19, 2021

I'm so ready to love the world
But I hate it for all it's not

November 23, 2021

Unku 36

Addictions
Tensegrity
Chains that suspend me

November 25, 2021

If you care
Then end your eye candy cameos
Put away your gratuitous sex scenes
Send away your half-naked cheerleaders
Let the buck stop here

November 27, 2021

Here's another girl
Who could've been mine forever
If she hadn't been everyone else's
For short periods of time

November 28, 2021

Haiku 69

Lord, I'm in a bind
Should I shame and embarrass
Or call him a her

Unku 37

Saving Lord
Grant him mercy
Or stupidity

December 2, 2021

Lady Liberty looked down
At her tiny feet
And all at once realized
This wasn't her dismembered body
But it was her choice

December 8, 2021

Haiku 70

I can only hope
Lennon revises his song
Before we arrive

December 17, 2021

I understand me
But in a pro-choice vegan world
No one else makes sense

December 18, 2021

Stop looking for the one
She died before birth
Or lived in ancient Babylon
Or a millennium yet to come
Speaking a language you don't know
Married to a man who is not you
With children who are not yours
She is the one in trillions—
the one most compatible
And the chances that she is now and here

Are approximately zero
But I have a dog
And from the first
We knew each other well
She is the best dog
Because I am hers
And she is mine
And I don't need any other
I think marriage should be as simple

December 23, 2021

Unku 38

Donald Trump
Look, Gideon
He drinks like a dog

December 26, 2021

JoeBad

Behold a good heart—
a man whose girls cry for joy
when he arrives home

Ready Player One

Search into the mind of your Creator
Know, love, serve
But it's still a game—
Truly your own game
And it's supposed to be fun
You've lost sight of that…
You wanted to win the race
You've been fighting the good fight
But remember the garden
Where there are no losers
Don't forget
That there was no race or fight
That you were created by Love
That before a leap of faith was required
    You could fly
    And walk on water
Don't forget that the city this place has become
Was built on a beautiful land
That even now, deserts can become fertile
And your part to play
Is not to buy and be sold
Nor to use and be used
Not even to win
But to love

January 13, 2022

The Tender Bar

My dog looks at every new question
With urgency and great concern
And upon finding she can't understand
Just goes about her business
Family life is for the simple and selfless
Who love the moment and live in it
Who take misfortune in stride
And don't need all the answers
Because home is good